Abide in The Word

A Practical Guide to Studying Scripture

Beth Wells

Inscript

Abide in the Word

Copyright 2025 by Beth Wells

All rights reserved

Paperback ISBN 978-1-957497-64-8

Inscript and the portrayal of a pen with script are trademarks of Dove Christian Publishers.

Published in the United States of America

Contents

ACKNOWLEDGMENTS

First and foremost, I thank God for giving my life purpose, for guiding me on His path, and for bringing people into my life who led me to the saving knowledge of Jesus Christ.

Thank you to Shane, whose love and support continually inspire me. He has been a wonderful partner, allowing me the freedom to change direction and follow God's plan… even when it hasn't been easy, He is the best roadie ever!

To my sisters and brothers in Christ, too many to name, who have encouraged me along the way and held me accountable, I deeply appreciate all the love you have poured into my life.

WHY ABIDE?

*I*n John 8:31, Jesus tells those who had believed Him, *"If you abide in my word, you are truly my disciples."*

But what does it really mean to "abide" and how do we do it?

Let's begin by understanding the word itself. In the original Greek, *abide* means "to stay in a given place, state, relation, or expectancy." Synonyms include *remain, lodge, dwell, continue,* and *endure.* Clearly, Jesus was calling us to something deeper than simply reading the Word; He wants us to live in it.

There is a vast difference between casually reading the Bible and truly studying Scripture. And it's through study – intentional, prayerful engagement with the Word - that we learn to truly *abide* in it. Before we dive into practical study methods, it's important to understand what the Bible actually is and why it's worthy of our time and devotion.

The Bible is not just one book, but a collection of 66 books, written by 40 men over a span of 1500 years, in three languages, and on three continents. Despite this diversity, it tells one unified story. Such consistency across time and geography is undeniable evidence of divine inspiration. The Bible was completed almost

2000 years ago, yet it is just as applicable today as it was then, proving what Jesus said in Matthew 24:35: *"Heaven and earth will pass away, but My words will never pass away."*

Let's go a little deeper.

2 Timothy 3:16 tells us that *"All Scripture is breathed out by God."* That same breath shows up in Genesis chapter 2, when God breathed life into Adam. The breath that gave us life is the same breath that gave us the Scriptures.

Hebrews 4:12 affirms that *"the Word of God is living and active."* The Bible is alive and powerful! But how can a book be alive? Because it is more than ink on a page, it carries the very breath of God.

> the Word is not just about God, or from God...it IS God.

In Revelation 19:13, we see a vivid image of Jesus' return, riding a white horse, and the name by which He is called is *"The Word of God"*.

John 1:1 echoes this truth: *"In the beginning was the Word, and the Word was with God, and the Word was God."*

John goes on to say that *"all things were made through Him, and without Him was not anything made that was made."*

Back in Genesis, we see that God spoke the world into existence. He said, *"Let there be light,"* and there was light. His word creates, shapes, and gives life. So when Jesus said "Abide in my Word" and also said "Abide in me," He's saying the same thing, because He is the Word. That is how He can speak to us through His Word, because the Word is not just about God, or

Why Abide?

from God...it IS God!

When we abide (remain, dwell, endure) in the Word of God, we connect with God Himself. As we memorize Scripture, we are placing more of God into our hearts and minds. When we allow Jesus to shape our thoughts, we become more like Him.

John 15:4, "*Abide in me, and I in you. As the branch cannot bear fruit by itself unless it abides in the vine, neither can you, unless you abide in me.*"

Jesus calls His followers to "*Go therefore and make disciples of all nations.*" But discipleship starts with abiding. It starts with becoming more like Him so that others can see His life reflected in ours..

When the Word lives in us, He will also live through us.

So far, we've looked at what it means to abide and why God's Word is worth abiding in. But maybe you, or someone you know, wants more than theological truth; maybe you're looking for proof that Bible study makes a difference in real life. Is there scientific evidence that shows reading the Bible has any positive influence? I'm glad you asked, because The Center of Bible Engagement released a report, known as "The Power of 4", based on an eight-year study of over 100,000 people.

Their findings revealed something incredible: those who engaged with Scripture four or more times a week experienced real, measurable transformation in their lives.

Temptation decreased, emotional struggles lessened, and faith-driven actions increased significantly.

The study found that by engaging in the Bible four or more times a week, the odds of giving in to these temptations decrease:

- Drinking to excess: -62%
- Viewing pornography: -59%
- Having sex outside of marriage: -59%
- Gambling: -45%
- Lashing out in anger: -31%
- Gossiping: -28%
- Lying: -28%
- Overeating/mishandling food: -20%
- Overspending/mishandling money: -20%

They found that reading and reflecting on God's Word four or more times per week led to more peace and joy by reducing emotional struggles, such as:

- Feeling bitter: -40%
- Destructive thoughts (toward self or others): -32%
- Need to hide feelings: -32%
- Holding unforgiveness: -31%
- Feeling discouraged: -31%
- Experiencing loneliness: -30%
- Fear or anxiety: -14%

The research also found that spending four or more days every week in Scripture had the following positive effects on faith:

- Giving financially to a church: +416%
- Memorizing Scripture: +407%
- Discipling others: +231%
- Sharing their faith with others: +228%
- Giving financially to causes other than church: +218%

Why Abide?

Those results are amazing and underline what Scripture has said all along: God's Word changes us. It teaches, corrects, comforts, convicts, and equips.

It keeps us from giving in to temptation: *"I have hidden Your Word in my heart, that I might not sin against You"* Psalm 119:11.

It gives us hope and joy: *"Blessed is the man who walks not in the counsel of the wicked, nor stands in the way of sinners, nor sits in the seat of scoffers; but his delight is in the law of the LORD, and on His law he meditates day and night"* Psalm 1:1-2.

And it has a positive impact on our faith: *"All Scripture is breathed out by God and profitable for teaching, for reproof, for correction, and for training in righteousness, that the man of God may be complete, equipped for every good work."* 2 Timothy 3:16-17.

Lastly, know that studying Scripture is how we learn God's character, find His promises for our lives, and know what He requires from us as we follow Him more closely every day. When we abide in the Word, we open ourselves to a life of peace, purpose, and power, all rooted in the presence of Christ.

Source: Center for Bible Engagement (CBE) White Paper, *Bible Engagement as the Key to Spiritual Growth: A Research Synthesis (2012)*

PREPARING TO ABIDE

$\mathcal{B}$efore we get into the different ways to study the Bible, let's talk about something that's just as important: making the choice to do it. We live in a world full of distractions, responsibilities, and endless to-do lists. If we don't set aside intentional time to be with God in His Word, it likely won't happen at all. Abiding doesn't happen by accident; it happens when we make room for it.

> Set aside some "quiet time" to be with God.

It's important to schedule or set aside time intentionally to do your study, not just try to "fit it in". The truth is, if you don't make it a priority, something else will always take its place. The enemy doesn't want to see you deep in God's word, and so he will try whatever he can to pull you away from it.

Setting a regular time and sticking to it makes God a priority in your life. Let those around you know this is your time with God, so they can support and respect that commitment. I used to refer to this as my "quiet time," but I recently heard someone call it "quality time," and I really like that. I think it describes what I am doing better: spending quality time listening to God speak to me through His Word.

I personally prefer early morning; it sets the tone for my day and puts me in a thoughtful and worshipful state of mind. I know some people who have their study time in the evening, and that works well for them. There is no right or wrong here; the important thing is that you set aside a time that works with your schedule.

Next, you need to create a "sacred space". This can be a room with a desk or table to spread out on, or even just a corner chair with a Bible and notebook. What is important here is that it is a space that is set apart, that you use to connect with God, where you can fully focus on the task at hand. You may want to decorate your area with special pictures and scented candles, or you may want it to be minimalist and plain. Again, there is no right or wrong; make the space personal

Avoid life's distractions during your quiet time

and comfortable so that you will look forward to your time spent there. You want the space to be one that helps you to relax and meditate on the Word, somewhere you can feel free to have conversations with God and to deepen and strengthen your faith.

It is also very important to remove any distractions, anything that may interrupt your special time. That may mean silencing your phone (you can return calls and texts later) or making sure the kids have what they need for that time. That was the reason I started doing my study early, when my kids were still asleep, so I could be sure of not being interrupted. Now that they are grown, I have kept the practice of early morning study. You know better than anyone else what things may pull your attention away, so make sure that those things are taken care of before you start. Remember that small steps count...at first, you may not be able to make every day work, or every day may not be a deep study, and that's OK. Any time spent in the Word of God is time well spent.

Once you know what type of study you want to engage in, you will better know what kind of space you need and what tools you will need to be successful. Whether it is space to write, art supplies to create, or reference books to look up information, making sure you have what you will need before you start will help you stay focused on the task at hand. If you are constantly having to get up to grab a notebook or a pencil that you forgot, you will be causing your own distractions and discouragement when your time is not spent the way that you want.

Now that your space is set up the way you want, you have everything in place, and you are ready to begin, make sure to do one more step: pray. Prepare yourself every time you sit down to study the Word and ask God to open your heart to receive whatever message He has for you that day. The goal of setting aside a time and space for Bible study should not be to impress others or check a spiritual box; the goal should always be to listen for God's voice and to discern His will for our lives.

Abide in the Word

When our heart is surrendered, and our motive is right, God will speak into us and use us to advance His kingdom. We only need to be obedient to listen for His will and to act on it when the Holy Spirit moves us.

We study the Word not just to know more, but to know Him more.

Ways to Abide

*O*n the following pages, I will explain six different ways to study God's Word in a deep and meaningful way. Each of these study styles invites you to approach God's Word with a different posture, some with your heart open in reflection, others with your mind engaged in study, and still others with your hands expressing worship through creativity. You don't need to choose just one.

Take your time to prayerfully consider, as you read through, which method fits your personal style the best, and then give it a try. Or, if there are several that you like and you're not sure which is the best fit, try each one for a few weeks and see what you think. Let the Spirit lead you into the method that fits this season, or rotate through them as you grow.

Ultimately, the best study style is the one that you will use!

Recognizing the Voice of Scripture

Before diving into the study styles, we need to take a moment to explore the writing styles found in the Bible. Understanding the style in which a passage is written can help us interpret it correctly and apply it more wisely. God inspired the writing of

His Word in a variety of distinct literary styles to communicate in ways people would understand. These styles were familiar in the culture of the ancient world, and the original hearers would have known how to interpret each one for its intended purpose, much like we instinctively know how to engage with a novel, a biography, or a news article today.

Each of these forms comes together to create a beautiful, unified work, and some books even weave together two or more styles. The main types of writing found in Scripture are:

Law * Narrative * Poetry
Wisdom * Prophecy * Gospels
Parables * Epistles * Apocalyptic

Let's take a moment to look at how to read and respond to each one.

1. Law

Found primarily in Genesis, Exodus, Leviticus, Numbers, and Deuteronomy, the first five books of the Old Testament. These books are also mostly narrative. The purpose of "The Law" was to guide Israel in holiness, justice, worship, and community living. It reveals God's character, His standards, and our need for a Savior.

When we read these books, we need to keep in mind the historical and covenant context, that the Old Testament law was given to Israel. Even though we are no longer expected to keep the OT law today, we can still find moral principles that do still apply, such as God's value of justice or purity. It also helps us to appreciate our need for Jesus, look at it as a guidepost that points to Christ, who fulfilled the Law on our behalf.

To get the most out of it, ask yourself: "What does this teach me about God's holiness, and how does it reveal my need for grace?"

2. Narrative (Historical Storytelling)

Almost half of the Bible is considered narrative, or stories of God's people throughout history. These stories reveal how God works through real people in real events, often over long periods of time, and all of the small stories are a part of the overall story of creation, fall, redemption, and restoration.

You will find this writing style in the Old Testament in: Genesis, Exodus, Numbers, Joshua, Judges, Ruth, 1 & 2 Samuel, 1 & 2 Kings, 1 & 2 Chronicles, Ezra, Nehemiah, Esther, Job, Jeremiah, Ezekiel, Isaiah, Daniel, Jonah, and Haggai. In the New Testament: Matthew, Mark, Luke, John, and Acts. When you read these stories, be sure to observe the people, setting, and sequence. Notice what choices the characters make and what those choices lead to. Remember that just because someone did something in the Bible, it doesn't mean it was the right thing. Reading and reflecting on these sometimes-flawed people can help us to learn about ourselves, and it can be a great reminder that God restores the broken and uses them for His glory.

As you read, think about what is revealed about God's faithfulness and how you can relate to this person's journey.

3. Poetry

Found in Psalms, Song of Solomon, and parts of the prophets, poetry expresses emotion, worship, and truth in a deeply personal and artistic form through imagery and symbolic language. It connects the heart to God through that imagery with rhythm and repetition. The Psalms were specifically used as a book of prayers and usually set to music. Within the 150 Psalms, you can find different themes to connect to different circumstances and seasons of life, such as lament, praise, thanksgiving, wisdom, and others.

When you read Biblical poetry, let it guide your prayers or worship and lead you to relate to God in an emotional and authentic way. Focus on the imagery used and ask, "What feelings is this drawing out in me?" "How can I use these words to speak to God?"

4. Wisdom Literature

Found in Proverbs, Ecclesiastes, and Job, wisdom literature offers us principles for living a godly, thoughtful, and balanced life. It is full of practical truths that can help guide us as we follow God. This style of writing offers guidance and common sense, and as we apply what is taught, we learn how to have reverence for God. Proverbs contain general truths describing how life usually works. Ecclesiastes shows honest wrestling with life's questions, and Job teaches about faith and suffering. All of these books can give us guidance on how to make better choices and how to address the tough questions of life.

> As you read Wisdom literature, ask yourself, *"What life principle can I carry into today from this?" "What is the lesson underneath the words?"*

5. Prophecy

In the Old Testament, we find the "major" prophets: Isaiah,

Jeremiah, Lamentations, and Ezekiel, and the "minor" prophets: Hosea, Joel, Amos, Obadiah, Jonah, Micah, Nahum, Habakkuk, Zepheniah, Haggai, Zechariah, and Malachi. The terms major and minor refer to the length of their books, not the quality of their content. And in the New Testament: Revelation. God chose people throughout the recorded history of the Bible to communicate messages from Himself to the people. There were many more prophets than the ones whose names are associated with books; the Old Testament prophets, with a few exceptions, were directed mainly to the nation of Israel, while Revelation is written to the New Testament Church.

The messages brought by the prophets were to communicate God's Law, Promises, and Sovereignty. They reminded the Israelites of the covenant they agreed to, pointed out the sins of the people and called them to repentance, and warned of the coming judgment if they failed to listen and obey. They also foretold future events, some about the immediate future of Israel and surrounding nations, and some about His plan of salvation for the world (Jesus), which have already been fulfilled. And Revelation, which gives prophecies about the second coming of Jesus that have yet to happen.

> As you read through the books of prophecy, look for the patterns of sin, judgment, repentance, and restoration. Ask: *"How is God calling His people, and me, back to Himself in this passage?"*

Even though most of these were written at a specific time for a specific audience, we can still find applications for ourselves. They can deepen our trust in God as we see His hand at work over time and give us confidence that He keeps His promises. The books of prophecy also give us a very clear understanding of God's character, who He is, and what He expects from us.

6. Gospels

Matthew, Mark, Luke, and John tell the gospel (the "good news") of Jesus' life, ministry, death, and resurrection. Each presents a unique perspective, but together they tell one unified story. Matthew presents Jesus as the long awaited Jewish Messiah, the fulfillment of Old Testament prophecy; Mark shows Him as the suffering Son of God, offering himself as a sacrifice for sins; In Luke, Jesus is the Savior for all, bringing salvation to every nation and people group; and John writes about Jesus as the eternal Son of God who came to bring eternal life to all who believe.

In addition to being biographies of Jesus' life, the gospels also include many of His teachings and bear witness to Him as the Son of God, the prophesied Messiah. As you read, look closely at Jesus' words, actions, and interactions, and see what they show about His heart for people, His authority, and His mission. Notice how people respond to Him, and how you are being invited to respond.

As you read the Gospels, ask yourself: *"What does this show me about Jesus? What would it look like for me to follow Him in this?"*

7. Parables

Found throughout the Gospels, especially in Matthew and Luke, parables are stories and illustrations that Jesus used to teach spiritual truths about the nature of God's kingdom. These stories often have more impact when you understand the references, which can sometimes be difficult 2000 years later! This is why it's important to look at who the original audience was and what the lesson would have meant to them. Also, look for ways to apply the lessons personally. Jesus often ended with a challenge or call to action. By using parables instead of just speaking plainly, Jesus engaged people's imaginations, encouraging them to think deeper, and ask questions to discover the answers for themselves, and they can do the same for us today. As you read, ask: "What is Jesus trying to reveal about the Kingdom of God, and how should that change me?"

8. Epistles (Letters)

Twenty-one of the Twenty-seven books of the New Testament are personal letters written by the apostles to individual believers or churches in the first century: Romans, 1 & 2 Corinthians, Galatians, Ephesians, Philippians, Colossians, 1 & 2 Thessalonians, 1 & 2 Timothy, Titus, Philemon, Hebrews, James, 1 & 2 Peter, 1, 2 & 3 John, and Jude

While the Gospels focused on what Jesus did, the letters explain the significance of those events, giving practical instruction for Christian living and providing guidance to the leaders of the early church. Some of the epistles were written to address situations that needed correction, such as misunderstandings or false doctrine. They also address the more general themes of following Christ for the whole church.

As you read, pay attention to context: who wrote it, to whom, and why? Notice that many of the letters begin with theology and end with application.

As you read, pay attention to context: who wrote it, to whom, and why? Notice that many of the letters begin with theology and end with application. Also, look for words or themes that are repeated. Ask yourself: "What truth is being taught here, and how does it affect the way I live and love others?"

9. Apocalyptic

Found mainly in Daniel and Revelation and also parts of Ezekiel, this is prophecy that uses vivid symbols and visions revealing spiritual realities and future events, specifically as they relate to the end of times when Jesus returns to Earth. They speak of spiritual warfare and describe events that take place on Earth from the perspective of Heaven. Although these writings can sometimes be difficult to understand, they are an important piece of the big picture, showing that evil will be judged, that God has the ultimate victory over Satan, and that believers are secure in their salvation. The truths in these books should give Christians

> As you read the Apocalyptic texts, take note of what the text tells you about the power and sovereignty of God.

an urgency to share the gospel message of Christ with others and help us to understand that God has control over all of His creation.

Understanding the literary styles of Scripture helps us do more than just read the Bible; it helps us listen for God's voice within it. Each style offers a different tone, rhythm, and purpose, but together they reveal the consistent, loving heart of our Creator. Whether we're reading the laws He gave to His people, the stories of those who walked with Him, the poetry of praise, or the letters of encouragement and instruction, God is speaking. When we learn how to recognize the style, we're better equipped to recognize His voice.

Now that we've explored the forms in which the Bible speaks, we're ready to dive into practical ways to study it. Let's begin exploring the tools and approaches that can help us truly abide in the Word.

CREATIVE JOURNALING/VERSE ILLUSTRATION

I used to think that studying the Bible always meant sitting down with a highlighter and a thick commentary, and sometimes it still does. But over time, I discovered that some of the richest moments in God's Word came when I slowed down, focused on just a few verses, and let them really speak to my heart.

That's what creative journaling allows us to do, to linger in the Word and respond personally. It isn't about being artistic or impressive; it's about making space for God to speak and then expressing what we hear in whatever way feels most meaningful. Maybe that means writing out a verse in beautiful lettering, sketching an image that comes to mind, or simply jotting down a quiet prayer.

If you've ever underlined a verse or written a note in the margin of your Bible, you've already started. Creative journaling gives us a chance to meet God in both stillness and expression, to dwell, reflect, and remember. It's a gentle way to abide.

Now that you know what creative journaling is, let's talk about how to get started. This kind of Bible study doesn't require fancy supplies or artistic talent. What it does require is a willing heart and a little space to listen.

Whether you're a seasoned journaler or this is your very first time, the steps are simple and adaptable. Think of this as a flexible framework, not a formula, a way to engage deeply with God's Word in a way that feels personal and prayerful.

<u>Supplies and Setup</u>

One of the first decisions you'll want to make is whether you want to use your everyday Bible for journaling or keep a separate Bible just for illustration. Some people create full-page paintings that cover the text, which can be beautiful, but may make certain verses unreadable. If that's the route you choose,

A journaling Bible works well for notes and drawings

it's a good idea to have a second Bible for reading and study. Personally, I prefer using my everyday Bible, so I avoid using any materials that obscure the text. A journaling Bible works well for this, one with wide margins that has room for notes and drawings. If you're using a regular Bible, you can still get creative by utilizing blank areas at the ends of chapters or around the text.

If you're not quite comfortable writing or illustrating directly in your Bible, that's perfectly fine; you can absolutely use a separate journal or sketchbook for your creative reflections. Some people even prefer having a dedicated notebook for this kind of study, a place where they can experiment freely, write prayers, or return to verses later. The goal isn't where you create, but that you take the time to pause, reflect, and respond to God's Word in a way that's meaningful to you.

For tools, I recommend starting simple: a mechanical pencil (no sharpening needed), and a set of colored pencils. I use Crayola Twistables for the same reason: they're easy and clean. I began with a basic 8-color set but later upgraded to 24 colors as I wanted to add more detail and depth to my drawings.

If you are working in the Bible that you will be using to read, you will definitely want to use colored pencils, which allow you to extend beyond the margin onto the text without obscuring the text or bleeding through the page. But if you're working in a separate Bible or journal, you can explore paints, pens, or markers.

The Process

Creative journaling is about meditating on the Word and responding in a way that helps you remember and reflect.

> **Basic steps to Creative Journaling:**
> 1. Read a passage and reflect on its meaning.
> 2. Choose specific words or a verse that stands out to you, that takes hold of your heart.
> 3. Visualize the verse – what image, symbol, or phrase comes to mind?
> 4. Sketch your idea lightly in pencil, meditating on the verse as you work.
> 5. Add color, details, or embellishments to complete your page.

There are many different ways that you may decide to illustrate the particular word, verse, or passage that you chose.

Decorative Lettering

Write out the verse using **creative lettering** and add embellishments like vines or flowers. If you're unsure how to start, there are lots of helpful lettering tutorials online. Remember that it doesn't have to be perfect; it's a special moment between you and God. Something that you can use as a reminder of the meaning of the verse when you see it. I especially love illustrating Psalms this way. There is a verse that is repeated in quite a few of the Psalms, "Give thanks to the LORD, for He is good, for His steadfast love endures forever. I have illustrated this verse three times, so far, in different ways and designs each time. Every time I see it, I am reminded of a song of worship, and I sing it as I draw.

Illustration

Draw a picture inspired by the verse. For example, one of my first illustrations came about during a sermon series on John 15, where Jesus says, "I am the vine and you are the branches…" I started by sketching a grapevine in the margin and then extending the vines across the page around the text. I later added color. Along with the highlights I made in the passage, that small sketch reminds me of the truths I learned from those sermons every time I see it.

Paraphrased Truths

Sometimes I'll write a phrase that sums up the message the passage speaks to me. In Habakkuk 2:3b says, *"If it seems slow, wait for it: it will surely come, it will surely come, it will not delay."* and verse 4b, *"the righteous shall live by faith."* I illustrated the idea: "Faith in God includes faith in His timing." That exact phrase was not in the text, but it's what God impressed on my heart as I studied.

Prayer Responses

Sometimes it is a prayer written in the margin next to a passage that comes to mind as I meditate on the words, a response to what God is showing me, or a request to help me live it out.

Let me encourage you: your illustrations won't look like anyone else's, and they're not supposed to. They're a reflection of your walk with God. That's what makes them beautiful.

> Your illustrations are unique and are a reflection of your walk with God. That's what makes them beautiful.

If you're ever feeling stuck for ideas, try searching online for "Bible Journaling Illustration ideas." You'll find plenty of inspiration. I am also including a few of my own ideas in the appendix to help you get started.

I absolutely love this form of Scripture study. For me, it is also an act of worship. I often sing as I draw, and each picture becomes a visual reminder of what God has spoken into my life. When I turn the pages of my Bible and see the illustrations, I don't just remember the artwork...I remember the moment I heard His voice.

Reflection Challenge

Choose a verse that has been meaningful to you this week. Read it slowly and reflect on what God is saying through it. Then, create a simple illustration or word art in the margin of your Bible or journal. Don't focus on making it perfect – focus on making it personal. Let it be a time of worship.

Character Study

Often when we think about Bible study, we picture reading a passage or diving into a topic. But sometimes the most powerful insights come from studying the people in Scripture. These weren't perfect saints living flawless lives; they were real men and women, no different than you and me. They experienced doubts, disappointments, temptations, and moments of bold faith. And through it all, God met them right where they were.

A character study invites us to slow down and walk beside someone in the pages of the Bible, to observe how they lived, what they believed, where they struggled, and how God worked in and through their lives. As we go deeper, we see that their stories aren't just ancient history, but that they are filled with timeless truth. The more we learn about them, the more we learn about ourselves and about the heart of God, who never changes.

You might be surprised to find out how much you can relate to someone like Ruth, who clung to hope in uncertainty... or Peter, whose impulsiveness was met with grace...or Joseph, who endured betrayal and waited patiently to see God's purpose unfold. Their lives become mirrors, mentors, and messages from Scripture, not just stories to read, but lives to learn from.

So how do we begin a character study? It's easier than you might think and deeply rewarding. You don't need a theology degree or a stack of commentaries. All you need is a Bible, a notebook, and a heart ready to listen. A study Bible with footnotes can be helpful for looking up extra information or using your favorite Bible app. By following a few intentional steps, you'll begin to see these individuals not as distant figures, but as people whose lives can speak directly into your own. Let's walk through the process together.

The first step is to choose a character; you can start with someone whose story you are already familiar with or ask God to lead you to someone unexpected. You may want to make a list of several people whose stories you want to explore, or let one naturally lead to another.

Once you have someone in mind, find and read the key passages where their story is told. A Bible app or concordance can help you locate all the places they're mentioned. As you read their story carefully, pay close attention to their actions, words, prayers, and responses to God.

It helps to keep some reflective questions in mind as you read. Some good questions are:

- What is this person's background?
- What challenges did they face?
- How did they respond to God?
- What do they reveal about God's character?
- What can I apply from their story to my own life?

Character Study

You're welcome to create your own questions or use the worksheet provided in the appendix at the back of the book.

Take notes as you read, write down key verses, character traits, moments of growth or failure, and significant quotes or interactions. You may want to sketch a simple timeline or create a chart to keep track of events and spiritual turning points. If you choose someone with a brief story, you can probably complete your study in one or two sittings. If you choose someone like Paul or Moses, whose stories are long and involved, you may take a couple of weeks to really find all of the nuances and explore their life fully, and that's OK. Take your time. Let the Holy Spirit move and speak to you through the process.

After your study, take a moment to reflect in prayer. Let God guide you in your reflections as you seek to find how this person's journey connects with your own. Ask "What do You want me to learn from this person's life?" This is where head knowledge becomes heart transformation.

One of my favorite character studies was the Woman at the Well; her story holds a special place in my heart for several reasons. She was an unlikely candidate to be a messenger of the Gospel, a sinful Samaritan woman with a complicated past. But  none of that mattered to Jesus. He saw her true heart. What I learned from her was that God can use us no matter who we are, what we have done, or where we have been. If we can open ourselves and recognize Jesus for who He truly is, we too can become vessels for sharing His Word. Her brief appearance in John's account left a lasting impact on me.

Just like other study styles, there is no "right" way to do this. It's your personal journey of discovery and connection. When you approach with an open heart and a willingness to listen, God will meet you right where you are, and you will find just what you need, no matter what season of life you are in.

 ## Reflection Challenge

Choose one person from the Bible. Read two or more passages from their life and write down:

- One thing you admire about them.
- One way their story challenges you.
- A prayer in response to what you have learned and how it applies to your life.

THEMATIC/TOPICAL STUDY

Sometimes, rather than studying a single passage or following one person's story, what we need most is to explore what the Bible says about a specific topic. Whether it's peace in a season of anxiety, wisdom for a big decision, or a deeper understanding of God's love, topical and thematic studies help us trace powerful truths throughout Scripture. These kinds of studies allow us to gather different verses that speak into one idea, helping us see both the big picture and personal application.

What's beautiful about this kind of study is that it meets you right where you are. If there's something you've been wrestling with, wondering about, or just feel curious to understand more fully, chances are God has already addressed it in His Word. The Bible is rich with themes...faith, forgiveness, strength, purpose... and as we search, reflect, and connect the dots, we begin to see how every part of Scripture works together to reveal God's heart and His consistent message throughout Scripture. Instead of staying in one passage, this study takes you across multiple books and authors to trace how the Bible addresses that particular topic.

Topical or thematic study doesn't require a special Bible

31

degree or a library of resources, just a willing spirit and a desire to learn. The process is simple, flexible, and entirely personal. You can spend one quiet evening exploring a handful of verses or dig in over several weeks. The key is to let the Word lead, and to follow where it points you, finding ways to apply its teachings to everyday life.

Let's walk through the basic steps to help you get started.

For this study, you will need a notebook and either a concordance, a study Bible with a topical index, or a Bible app

Start by choosing a topic. Pray for direction and ask God to lead you to one that will speak into your heart. Choose something you want to know more about, like "joy" or "faith", or something you are struggling with, like "anxiety" or "anger." Or you can study biblical themes like covenant, redemption, or holiness. Or more personal ones like identity, healing, or obedience.

> Let the Word lead, and follow where it points you, finding ways to apply its teachings to everyday life.

Using your reference book or app, look for key verses or passages that address your theme or topic directly. It's important to study verses in their full context to avoid misinterpretation. Look for patterns, repeated words or phrases, commands, promises, or characteristics of God

As you read, keep some questions in mind, such as:

- What does this reveal about God?
- What does this teach about people?
- How does this apply to my life?

Thematic/Topical Study

Write a paragraph (or a page!) summarizing what you've learned about your chosen topic or theme. Make a commitment to take action in applying what you have found, let what you've learned shape your decisions, attitude, or spiritual practice. As always, conclude your study time with prayer, thanking God for guiding you through your study time and for revealing Himself to you.

There are so many themes/topics in Scripture; don't worry if your list of verses seems long. Take your time! Remember that you don't have to study every verse on a topic at once; let it unfold over time. Try focusing on one topic per week or even one per month, and find a pace that works for you.

Let's walk through an example together so you can get the full idea: Let's say you've chosen *spiritual warfare* as your theme. It's a topic that feels especially relevant when we're walking through spiritual battles, discouragement, temptation, or facing opposition in our faith.

Step 1: Pray and Ask God to Lead You

Before opening your Bible, ask the Lord to give you understanding and to speak through His Word.

Step 2: Gather Scriptures

You might start with verses like:

- **Ephesians 6:10-20** – The armor of God
- **2 Corinthians 10:3-5** – Tearing down strongholds
- **James 4:7** – "Resist the devil, and he will flee from you"
- **1 Peter 5:8-9** – Be alert and of sober mind
- **Romans 8:37-39** – Nothing can separate us from the love of God
- **Matthew 4:1-11** – Jesus' temptation in the wilderness

Step 3: Study Each Passage in Context

Take time to read the surrounding verses. As you do ask:

- What does this say about the battle we face?
- What is God's role? What is mine?
- Are there any commands, promises, or truths to cling to?

Step 4: Look for Patterns and Truths

Notice repeated themes like *standing firm, resisting the enemy,* and *relying on God's strength.* Many passages also emphasize knowing the Word as a key defense, just as Jesus did in the wilderness.

Step 5: Apply and Summarize

"Spiritual warfare is real, but I am not powerless. God equips me with truth, righteousness, peace, faith, salvation, and His Word. My job is to stand firm, stay alert, and fight not in my own strength but through prayer and Scripture. I don't fight for victory, I fight *from* victory."

Step 6: Respond in Prayer

End your study with a prayer asking God to help you apply what you've learned, to equip you with His armor, and to strengthen you in any battles you're currently facing.

Reflection Challenge

Choose a theme that speaks to your current season, such as joy, fear, grace, or purpose. Look up 3 -5 Bible verses on that topic. Then:

- Write one sentence that summarizes what you learned.
- Reflect on how this truth applies to your life today.
- Write a short prayer asking God to help you live out what you've discovered.

VERSE MAPPING

*S*ometimes a single verse stops us in our tracks, whether it's deeply encouraging, hard to understand, or rich with truth we don't want to miss. Verse mapping is a way to slow down and really sit with that verse, to dig deeper into the language, context, and meaning so that God's Word can take root in our hearts. It's like a word-study road map, and it's not about speed or quantity; it's about quality. It helps us uncover the layers of Scripture, making connections we might otherwise overlook. If you enjoy detailed study or just want to learn how to get more out of your Bible time, this may become one of your favorite ways to abide in the Word.

Whether you're studying a familiar verse or exploring something new, this process will guide you to observe, understand, and apply God's truth more intentionally. Because this method involves a more detailed study, it does require a few extra resources for research. A Bible dictionary or lexicon, a concordance, your favorite commentary, and of course your Bible and a notebook. These days, there are amazing resources online, so you don't need to take up space with large books, but if you're old-school like me, you may enjoy flipping through the pages to find what you need.

This method is a bit more involved, so I'm going to walk through an example of how to do it as I explain the steps. Let's go!

For this Verse Mapping walk-through, I chose Philippians 4:6.

Step 1: Write the Verse

Start by writing out the verse by hand; this helps you slow down and notice every word.

> "Do not be <u>anxious</u> about anything, but in everything by prayer and supplication with thanksgiving let your <u>requests</u> be made known to God."

Choose at least two alternate translations and compare them with your main verse; see where the wording varies and underline or highlight the differences. Different translations help uncover emphasis; some use "anxious," others "worried." This can help you understand what the verse is really saying.

> **New Living Translation (NLT):** "Don't <u>worry</u> about anything; instead, pray about everything. Tell God what you <u>need</u>, and thank Him for all He has done."

> **New International Version (NIV):** "Be <u>careful</u> for nothing; but in every thing by prayer and supplication with thanksgiving let your requests be made known unto God."

Step 2: Highlight & Define Key Words

Choose several keywords that seem central to the verse, maybe ones that you want to know more about, and write the definition of each. Use the concordance to find original Greek or Hebrew words. If it helps you to keep track of things, you may want to color-coordinate the words and their definitions using highlighters or colored pencils. For this verse, I pulled out the following:

- **Anxious** – to be pulled in different directions; to worry; to be distracted; excessive worry or concern about the future, especially when it leads to a lack of trust in God's provision and care.
- **Prayer**- communication with God, encompassing various forms like supplication, confession, thanksgiving, and adoration. It's expressing our hearts and minds to God and also listening for His guidance.
- **Supplication** – A form of prayer characterized by humility and earnestness, involving a heartfelt and specific request for help or favor from God. A humble plea or entreaty, often stemming from a sense of need or desperation, emphasizing the believer's dependence on God's grace and mercy.
- **Thanksgiving** – A heartfelt expression of gratitude to God for His goodness, blessings, and provision, often demonstrated through praise, worship, and acts of obedience.
- **Requests** – An act of asking God for something through prayer or supplication, encompassing various forms of expression, including petition, entreaty, and seeking guidance. Often implying faith, humility, and a desire to align with God's will.

By looking up the definitions, you begin to see that this verse isn't just about praying in general, it's about shifting your mental state from anxious thoughts to trust-filled requests and doing it with gratitude. Finding the full definitions helps you to understand the meaning more deeply and better find ways to apply the truths in the words.

Step 3: Context

Read the surrounding verses:

> *"Rejoice in the Lord always; again I will say, rejoice. Let your reasonableness be known to everyone. The Lord is at hand;"* - Philippians 4:4-5

> *"And the peace of God, which surpasses all understanding, will guard your hearts and your minds in Christ Jesus."* -Philippians 4:7

Do some research and find out who wrote the passage, when, and to whom. Paul wrote this particular advice from prison, reminding believers to rejoice and trust. That adds weight to his words. We can also see from the context what Paul says our state of mind should be (always rejoicing in the Lord), and also that if we follow the form of prayer he outlines, it leads to a promise from God to fill us with His peace.

<u>Step 4: Cross-References</u>

Find at least three other verses that speak to the same topics. In this case, I'm looking for verses about worry, prayer, or God's peace:

> **Matthew 6:25-34** – *Jesus says not to worry about your life because your Heavenly Father knows what you need and will take care of you.*

> **1 Peter 5:7** – *"Cast all your anxieties on Him, because He cares for you."*

> **Colossians 4:2** *"Continue steadfastly in prayer, being watchful in it with thanksgiving."*

Throughout Scripture, we find the theme of prayer with thankfulness as a remedy for anxiety; this shows the consistency of God's encouragement and promises.

<u>Step 5: Apply It</u>

It's time to ask some questions. Read over all of the information you have gathered, pray, and ponder, asking: *What does this verse reveal about God? What does it reveal about me? What is God asking me to do?*

- God invites me to bring everything to Him in prayer.
- I'm not meant to carry my worries alone.
- Thankfulness should be part of my daily prayers.
- There is peace on the other side of surrender.

Finish your study by writing out a short response prayer based on what you've learned:

Father God, help me trade worry for worship. Let me come to You quickly with every concern and not forget to thank You for what You've already done. Teach me to trust that You hear every request and that peace is always possible when I'm anchored in You. Amen.

Verse mapping gives us the opportunity to move beyond surface reading and really immerse ourselves in the heart of Scripture. It helps us slow down and savor the richness of God's Word, one verse at a time. As you explore keywords, consider context, and connect other passages, you'll begin to see how powerfully the Bible speaks into your everyday life. The more time you spend mining the depths of a single verse, the more personal and transformative your time with God will become. As you become more comfortable with the process, you may want to add some creativity to your pages, like fancy lettering and colors. Let this method be a tool that helps you not only understand the Word but also abide in it.

 ## Reflection Challenge:

Choose one verse that has been on your heart lately – or one that speaks to a current situation in your life. Use the steps of verse mapping to dig deeper and reflect. Then, write:

- A key truth or insight you discovered
- One cross-reference verse added depth of clarity.
- A personal prayer based on what God revealed to you.

LINE-BY-LINE (VERSE-BY-VERSE) STUDY

*T*here's something powerful about slowing down. In a fast-paced world full of quick reads and instant answers, line-by-line study invites us to pause and soak in every word of Scripture. It's about savoring, not speed. When we move carefully through a passage, sentence by sentence, we begin to notice the richness of God's truth in a way we might otherwise overlook.

This kind of study helps us break down the structure and flow of a passage. We learn to look closely, not just at what is being said, but how it's being said. By asking questions, noting repetition, observing transitions, and reflecting on why each phrase matters, Scripture becomes more than a message; it becomes a conversation.

Line-by-line study is a simple yet powerful method for anyone seeking to deepen their understanding of God's Word. In this method, we also take into consideration the full context of when and to whom the words were written. There are many references in Scripture that were instantly understood by the people of the time, but that are not quite as clear to us today. There are also changes in some word meanings as language evolves over time. It's important to remember that while the Bible was written *for* us, it was not written *to* us. By learning about the customs and culture of the times, we can find a much deeper and truer understanding of what we read.

A line-by-line study isn't complicated, but it does take patience and intention. It's more than simply reading; it's interacting with the text. As you walk slowly through each verse, you'll ask questions, look for meaning, and allow the Holy Spirit to guide your thoughts. Whether you're studying a single paragraph or an entire chapter, this approach helps you engage deeply with God's Word, one line at a time. Let's walk through the process together.

> The Bible was written *for* us, it was not written *to* us.

To get set up for this method, you will need a few things. Of course, a notebook and your Bible, add to that a concordance and a commentary or two. As before, these things are readily available online if you prefer.

Choose a short passage; five to ten verses is a great place to start. Narrative, poetry, letters, or even parables all work well for this style of study. As you become more comfortable, you will find it easier to apply to longer passages, chapters, or even working through entire books one verse at a time.

Read the passage all the way through once or twice to get the overall feel. Then prepare to slow down and take it one verse, one sentence, even one word, at a time.

Write out each verse as you go; this will help you to process the words more deeply. As you write each line in your notebook or journal, leave space underneath for notes. You can also leave larger margins for side comments.

For each line that you read and then write, ask reflective questions:

- What is being said?
- Who is speaking, and to whom?
- Are there any repeated words or themes?
- Is there a command or promise?
- Are there any words that may have changed in meaning over time?
- Does this reference a particular custom that may be different now than then?

Highlight or underline any words that stand out; these could be verbs, names, attributes of God, or terms that are central to the message. Pay attention to small connecting words that carry weight, like "therefore", "but", "so that."

Write down any questions that come up. If something is unclear, make a note of it so you can return to it or look up additional context later. Then, pause to reflect:

- What does this mean for me?
- How can I apply this truth today?

Find cross-references, other verses that relate to the key words or themes. This helps Scripture interpret Scripture and show how the Bible connects across books and authors. Many times, this step can give you a good bit of additional insight and bring more understanding.

After you've gone through the passage line-by-line, write a short summary of what you've learned or what stood out most. Then respond with a prayer, a written reflection, or an action step.

Here is a sample walk-through of a line-by-line study:

Philippians 2:1-5

Step 1: Read the passage slowly, let the words sink in as we prepare to go verse by verse.

Step 2: Write and Reflect

Verse 1. *"So if there is any encouragement in Christ, any comfort from love, any participation in the Spirit, any affection and sympathy,"*

Observation: Paul is asking rhetorical questions, implying that these things do exist among believers.

Key Words: encouragement, comfort, participation, affection, sympathy.

Reflection: Am I experiencing these things in Christ? Am I offering them to others?

Verse 2. *"complete my joy by being of the same mind, having the same love, being in full accord and of one mind."*

Observation: Unity is Paul's deep desire for the church.

Key Words: same mind, same love, full accord.

Reflection: How am I contributing to unity in the Body of Christ?

Verse 3. *"Do nothing from selfish ambition or conceit, but in humility count others more significant than yourselves."*

Observation: A clear command paired with a Christlike mindset of how we are to treat others.

Key Words: nothing, selfish ambition, humility, more significant.

Reflection: Where do I struggle with selfishness? How can I practice humility?

Verse 4. *"Let each of you look not only to his own interests, but also to the interests of others."*

Observation: We aren't told to neglect ourselves, but not to stop at ourselves.

Key Words: not only...but also

Reflection: Who has God placed in my life that I can serve or care for more intentionally?

Verse 5. *"Have this mind among yourselves, which is yours in Christ Jesus,"*

Observation: Paul is calling us to imitate Christ's attitude, which we already have access to

Key Words: this mind, yours in Christ.

Reflection: Am I living like I have the mind of Christ available to me?

Step 3: Summarize and Respond

Summary: Paul is calling the church to live in humble unity, putting others first, and modeling the attitude of Christ.

Prayer: *Father God, give me a heart of humility. Help me to look beyond myself and reflect Your love in how I serve others.*

Action Step: Identify one person this week I can intentionally encourage or serve in love.

Bible Journaling

Sometimes, the best way to stay consistent in our study is to follow a simple, repeatable method, and that's where Bible Journaling with acronyms can be a powerful tool. These methods provide structure without stifling personal reflection. Whether you're new to studying Scripture or looking to go deeper, acronym-based journaling helps you slow down, focus your thoughts, and make meaningful connections. These models guide us through a process of reading, reflecting, and responding to God's Word in a way that makes it personal and applicable. Each step invites us to engage with Scripture, not just for information, but for transformation.

There are many simple acronym-based models you can explore; each offers a slightly different approach to interacting with Scripture. Here are a few you might want to look at:

- **J.O.Y.** (Just write it, Observe what you see, Your heart's response)

  A gentle, creative approach that encourages you to reflect honestly and personally on what you've read.
- **P.O.W.E.R.** (Prayer, Observe, Write, Envision, Response)

This method begins with prayer and helps you envision how Scripture applies to your life before responding to God.

- **P.S.A.L.M.** (Paraphrase, Study, Analyze, Learn, Meditate) A rich study format that walks you through a deeper understanding and meditation on the passage.
- **S.O.A.P.** (Scripture, Observation, Application, Prayer) One of the most popular and widely used journaling methods, S.O.A.P. helps you apply God's Word in a practical way and end your study in prayer.

Each of these tools provides a thoughtful rhythm of study and reflection. You might find that different models work better for different seasons, topics, or passages. The goal isn't to follow a formula, but to open your heart to hear from God. My personal favorite is the **H.E.A.R.** method, and I'd love to walk you through the details of how it works and how it can transform your time in the Word.

> **H.E.A.R.** stands for **H**ighlight, **E**xplain, **A**pply, and **R**espond.

I use the H.E.A.R. method daily. I love this model because it not only helps you study Scripture in context but also challenges you to act on what you've learned. For this study, you will need your Bible, a notebook, and a commentary; a concordance can also be helpful.

To begin, choose a chapter to read through. You may want to work through an entire book, reading and journaling on one chapter per session. As you read, be open to the prompting of the Spirit and look for one or two verses that stand out to you. Once a verse speaks to your heart, you're ready to begin your journal entry.

H. (Highlight) Simply write out the verse you have chosen to focus on.

E. (Explain) Now comes the research: look at commentaries, word meanings, and context, and write out a paragraph or two on what this verse means. Who is speaking? Who are they speaking to? What brought them here, and what's going on in the surrounding passage? Try to find as much detail as you can to describe the action and draw out the spiritual truth in the words.

A. (Apply) Based on what you've learned, reflect on how you can apply this truth in your own life. Be specific. What steps can you take? Has there been a time you've already seen this truth at work?

R. (Respond) Take a moment to write a personal prayer in response to what you've studied. Thank God for the insight and ask for wisdom or strength to live it out.

Here is a sample of a completed H.E.A.R. Journal:

1 Kings 19:11-12

H. *And He said, "Go out and stand on the mount before the LORD." And behold the LORD passed by, and a great and strong wind tore the mountains and broke in pieces the rocks before the LORD, but the LORD was not in the wind. And after the wind an earthquake, but the LORD was not in the earthquake. And after the earthquake a fire, but the LORD was not in the fire. And after the fire the sound of a low whisper.*

E. Elijah has run into the wilderness to hide from Jezebel. He let the fear in his flesh overcome the courage and strength he had from God. Because of this, he was so discouraged that he even prayed for death, but God met him in that place, supplying food, water, and rest. The Angel of the LORD (Jesus Himself) came to him. Elijah then traveled 200 miles to Mount Horeb (also known as Sinai, the same place where Moses met God). God gave him this time to recover from spiritual exhaustion. Once he arrived, God asked him a question He knew the answer to, but He allowed Elijah to respond and so unburden his heart. Elijah felt isolated and alone, con-

vinced that no one else remained faithful. Then came the personal encounter: God showed him wind, earthquake, and fire, but He was not present in any of those things. Finally, He came in a "still small voice", the Hebrew says *a voice of gentle silence*. We often, like Elijah, expect God to move in dramatic ways, and sometimes He does, but more often He comes quietly. In that still small voice, God gave Elijah direction and reminded him of his purpose.

A. How often do I let my expectations of what I think my purpose is, or should be, lead me to be disappointed or discouraged? Like Elijah, I sometimes feel like I've missed something or failed somehow. But even in the midst of that, God is waiting for me to listen for His quiet whisper. The truth is that as long as I continue to draw breath, He still has a plan for me. I only need to yield myself, trust His timing, and be available to follow where He leads, even if the path is not what I had anticipated. He is not going to show me the whole story all at once. I have to continue to walk in faith as it unfolds one chapter, one page, even one sentence at a time, and trust that He will lead me where He wants me to be. God is always getting me ready for what comes next. I only need to step out in obedience with faith.

R. *Father God, please forgive me for the times I try to take control and get ahead of Your plan. I know that You have great things in store for me and that You desire to use me in a mighty way to further Your kingdom. Thank you for being patient with me as I continue to learn to listen for Your whisper and to faithfully follow where You lead. I want to be the clay in Your hands and allow You to shape me into a vessel that will accomplish Your will.*

 ## Reflection Challenge

Choose a chapter from one of the Gospels (Matthew, Mark, Luke, or John). As you read, ask the Holy Spirit to guide your heart and mind. When a verse stands out to you, use the H.E.A.R journal method to record your thoughts:

Highlight the verse by writing it out.

Explain what it means in its context

Apply it to your life today

Respond with a prayer

Take your time and be honest in your reflections. If you feel comfortable, repeat this process for several days in a row using different verses from the same Gospel. Notice how God speaks to you in new ways each time.

Abiding Daily: Letting the Word Dwell In You

You've spent time learning to engage with the Word of God in meaningful, creative, and intentional ways. Whether you journaled creatively, studied characters, or mapped out verses, each time you opened your Bible, you opened your heart to hear from God. But this journey doesn't end when the study closes or when the notebook pages are full; this is where it begins to truly take root.

To abide means to remain, and one of the most powerful ways we remain in God's Word is to carry it with us daily in our hearts as well as in our hands. The best way to carry His Word in our hearts is through Scripture Memorization.

Psalm 119:11 says, *"I have hidden your word in my heart, that I might not sin against you."*

Memorizing Scripture plants God's truth deep inside us, where it can grow, strengthen, and sustain us. It becomes our anchor in uncertainty, our defense in temptation, our comfort in sorrow, and our joy in praise.

When Jesus was tempted in the wilderness, He didn't pull

out a scroll; He spoke Scripture aloud. He had it ready in His heart, and the same can be true for us. Memorization gives us the tools we need to live, speak, and walk in truth, even when life gets loud or hard.

Memorization doesn't have to be complicated or overwhelming. Here are a few simple and effective ways to begin:

Start small – Choose short, meaningful verses that speak to you.

Write it down – Use a journal, sticky note, or index cards.

Speak it out loud – Add it to your prayer time or daily routine.

Display it – Post it on your mirror, fridge, or phone wallpaper.

Make it creative – Draw it, decorate it, sing it, whatever helps you connect!

Repeat often – Revisit the verse daily until it sticks.

Use it – Look for ways to speak it in conversation or prayer

Let this become part of your rhythm. One verse at a time, you are hiding His Word in your heart, and that's a powerful way to abide.

 ## Reflection Challenge

Choose one verse from a recent study, maybe it's a verse that comforted you, convicted you, or encouraged you. Write it out and commit to memorizing it this week. Speak it over yourself each morning. Pray it at night. Share it with a friend.

At the end of the week, take time to reflect:

- How has this verse shaped your thoughts or actions?
- How did God use it to speak to you?
- What did you learn about Him in the process?

Abiding Daily: Letting the Word Dwell In You

This book may be coming to a close, but your time abiding in God's Word is just beginning. Keep coming back. Keep making space.

Abiding isn't about perfection; it's about presence. It's about showing up with a willing heart and trusting that God will meet you there.

He always does.

"Let the Word of Christ dwell in you richly…" Colossians 3:16.

A Closing Prayer

Father God,

Thank you for meeting us in these pages and for the gift of Your living Word.

Thank you for every moment of stillness, every truth revealed, and every whisper of Your Spirit along the way. As we go forward, help us to remain in You, to abide in Your Word with open hearts, listening ears, and obedient lives.

Let Your truth take root in us and bear fruit that glorifies You.

Teach us to walk in Your ways, to speak with grace, to love with purpose, and to shine with the light of Christ in every season.

May the seeds planted here grow strong in faith and rich in wisdom.

And may Your Word dwell in us richly, guiding, shaping, and sustaining us day by day.

In the holy and precious name of Jesus, the Living Word,

Amen

APPENDIX: TOOLS FOR THE JOURNEY

*I*n this section, you will find practical worksheets and journaling prompts designed to help you apply the Bible study methods shared in this guide. Whether you're just beginning your study journey or looking for a fresh way to engage with Scripture, these pages are here to support you. There is no "one-size-fits-all" approach to drawing closer to God; these tools are flexible, personal, and meant to meet you right where you are. Use them to reflect, explore, and respond as the Holy Spirit leads. You can copy these pages and use them as they are, just "fill in the blanks," or use them as guidelines to help you develop your own personal style.

However you choose to proceed, I pray that these resources will be a blessing as you continue to abide in the Word.

Creative Journaling/ Verse Illustration

Appendix: Tools for the Journey

<u>Character Study Worksheet</u>

Character Name: _____

Key Scripture References: _____

Background Information:

Where are they from?

What time period did they live in?

What was their family or social status?

What are the major events in their life? (create a brief timeline if helpful)

Strengths/Positive Traits:

Weaknesses/Mistakes:

How did they respond to God?

What does their story teach me about:

God's character

Human nature

Abide in the Word

My own walk with God

One lesson I can apply to my life:

A prayer based on what I've learned:

Appendix: Tools for the Journey

Thematic/Topical Study Worksheet

Theme/Topic: _____

Why did I choose this topic?

Key questions I want answered:

Main Scripture passages (at least 3):
1.

2.

3.

What do these passages have in common?

What does this theme reveal about God?

How does this apply to my life?

Action steps or things to reflect on:

A verse I want to memorize from this study:

Appendix: Tools for the Journey

<u>Verse Mapping Worksheet</u>

Verse with reference:

Keywords (write out original meanings/definitions)

Additional translations:

Cross references:

Context Summary
Who

What

When

Where

Why

Abide in the Word

Personal Insight:

Life Application:

Response Prayer:

Appendix: Tools for the Journey

<u>Line-by-Line Study Worksheet</u>

Passage (Book, Chapter, Verses)

Breakdown:
Verse:
Summary:/observation

Keywords:

Application/reflection

Verse:
Summary/observation:

Keywords:

Application/reflection:

Verse:
Summary/observation:

Keywords:

Application/reflection:

Abide in the Word

Verse:

Summary/Observation:

Keywords:

Application/Reflection:

What is the main message of this passage?

What is my response? (prayer/action steps)

Appendix: Tools for the Journey

Bible Journaling Worksheet (H.E.A.R. Example)

H. (Highlight – write out the verse)

E. (Explain – Summarize the meaning)

A. (How does this apply to my life?)

R. (Respond with prayer or commitment)

REFERENCE & RECOMMENDED RESOURCES

These are some of the trusted study tools and reference books I personally use in my own time of Bible study and preparation. I encourage you to explore them as you grow in your understanding of God's Word.

- The New Strong's Exhaustive Concordance of the Bible – James Strong
- Rose Book of Bible Charts, Maps, and Timelines – Rose Publishing
- Charles H Spurgeon's Whole Bible Commentary – Charles Spurgeon
- The Wycliffe Bible Commentary – Charles F. Pfeiffer and Everett F. Harrison
- Matthew Henry's Commentary on the Whole Bible – Matthew Henry
- Blue Letter Bible App – www.blueletterbible.org
- Enduring Word Commentary by David Guzik – www.enduringword.com
- YouVersion Bible App

www.ingramcontent.com/pod-product-compliance
Lightning Source LLC
Chambersburg PA
CBHW050903120626
46554CB00003B/990